D1715937

My Beautiful Ruins

poems by

Craig Ciarán Lennon

TEAMPALL CHIARÁIN PRESS

CATSKILL, NEW YORK

Published in the United States by:

Teampall Chiaráin Press

P. O. Box 730, Catskill, New York 12414

Cover design: The Turning Mill, Palenville, New York 12463
Cover photo: taken by the author (Monastery of Clonmacnoise, County Offaly,
Ireland. Established by Irish Saint Ciaran in 544 AD.)
Lennon, Craig Ciarán
My Beautiful Ruins
ISBN: 978-0-9978964-0-4
1. Poetry

My Beautiful Ruins

CONTENTS

I. Innocence

II. The Past Is Not Dead

III. Shadows

IV. Awakening

V. Lamentation

VI. Loving Vessel

This book is dedicated to

Gerard Francis O'Rahilly

August 1, 1956 to April 24, 2014

Hero in his brokenness,
noble in his suffering
the tremendous voices in his head.
I witnessed the descent of his mind
into the dark affliction of schizophrenia
a spiritual teaching I struggle to understand
to this day.

Beannacht De le hanama na marbh.
Ta said imithe ar shli na firinne.

(the Gaelic Blessing of the Dead)

trans.

The blessing of God on the souls of the dead.
They are gone on the way of truth.

You must give birth to your images.
They are the future waiting to be born.
Do not fear the strangeness you feel,
The future must enter into you
Long before it happens.

—Rainer Maria Rilke
(from *Letters To A Young Poet*)

When inward tendency finds the secret hurt
Pain itself will crack the rock
And let the soul emerge.

—Jelaludin Rumi

My Beautiful Ruins

I.
Innocence

There was a time when
Meadow, grove and stream,
The earth and every common sight
To me did seem
Appareled in celestial light
The glory and freshness of a dream…

—William Wordsworth

I Am Ciarán

I am Ciarán.
The gods have been seeking me from the beginning.
As a child they initiated me into communion
with the shy whisper of trees,
mysterious dialects of the river,
accents of the wind sweeping over water.

As I grew older I drifted into the noise,
hid from the gods in my thoughts,
lost myself in the clouding,
forgot the language of the quiet sun
on the mountainside,
brushing its moody colors,
delicate as twilight.

Tonight the gods are taking me back.
The shell of my mind cracks open.
They enter through the secret cave of my heart.
Their desire for me
surges in my own blood
with a choir of voices reminding me

I am made of longing.

They descend
on the scaffolding of the stars,
enter the sacred doorways

at all the thin places,
gather in the corridors of the forest,
like a swelling melody of fireflies.

The wind and fire are married
in a towering spiral of gleaming flesh.
Flames leap in concert
with the ecstatic whirling of trees.
Even the slumbering mountains
wake up and glide through the valley,
like ancient tortoises floating in the moonlight,
singing their primeval melodies of
the first symphonies of light.

Tonight at the assembly of Being,
I am turning myself in,
casting off this old skin,
the way a tree throws off its burning colors
surrenders its radiance to the gods.

I am Ciarán
Made of longing.

Note: "I am made of longing" comes from a phrase used by
Rilke in *The Book of Hours*.

Original Light

I AM the original wave
that shimmered inside the longest night.
My first tremor of light
cut many universes deep,
opening a blessed wound,
luminous blood of birthing.

I flared forth like wind,
imagining a structure to embrace.
I am the ONE who dreamed love
into form,
bliss drenched the emptiness
with living flames.
Glistening, I moved upon the silence,
the vast symphony of a kiss.

I AM the absolute clarity
of the original light.
I AM moving inside,
in your mind, in your eyes,
in your blood,
in this breath,
in this moment.

Be still and know
as we move as one upon the silence,
I AM closer to you now
than your own heart beating
many universes deep.

Star Windows

One summer night
as this tiny earth rock
spun lazily through the Milky Way,
Ciarán stood in a meadow
watching fireflies ignite
their tiny furnaces,
dreams with wings,
luminous sailing ships,
untethered stars
seeking familiar light.

Mesmerized by the mystic art
of hide and seek
he tracked each flashing beacon
fleeing into the next universe
and slipping back in,
the captured light
of drifting lighthouses
glowing in the palm of his hands.
For one brilliant moment
reaching his hands to the sky,
a burning presence rested in the latticework
of his outstretched fingers.

Gazing deeply upon that fire
his vision penetrated through
the star windows,
beyond the ancient flames,
to the towering conflagration
behind all things.

Ciarán fell to his knees
with the unbearable multitude of lights
in his mind.
What was transmitted into him
in that moment
he cannot explain,
but it lives in him now
and in the one radiance
shining through all things.

The Gift of Flesh

I am Ciarán,
here from the beginning.
I am the hawk,
circling the ancient towers.
I am the shadow,
treacherous dark triangle
creeping over the meadow,
and the small creature's wariness of sky.
I am the shriek,
psychic arrow,
the white rabbit's
whiplash of black terror,
surging red blood,
feints and swerves,
the feverish scamper,
archaic memory of the ancestors,
relentlessly stalked
by the stealth shadow
passing over high grass,
and nowhere to hide.

I am the cruel crosshairs,
fierce angle of bloodlust,
strike of the spear,
the shape of horror as I close death's door.
I am the precise penetration,
beak and claw of annihilation,
purpose of blood,
the sorrow,
the gift of flesh,
holy communion of predator and prey.

I raise up the trembling body,
pierce it in the trees.
A radiant arc of clear light
rises skyward,
soars through towering white elegance,
beyond the monastery of stars.

Praying with Rain

One day you will lose yourself walking in the rain.
With one innocent step you will cross into the infinite.
With one new breath you will arrive in the eternal moment.
You may want to dance
or perhaps kneel and pray.
Either way you will be thrown off the throne
of your mind
into the deepening wellspring of you.

Listen closely to the dragon roar,
watch the light spears that split the sky
and cause the tears to flow.

See the tree's slender body
shimmering with pearls of rain,
fleshy leaves like hands folded in prayer.
From the roots to the treetop
a translucent gown of mist
has woven itself around the branches
like a wreath of flames.

In the steady prayer of rain
the secret one will rinse your mind
with formlessness,
cleanse the deepest wounds
like the dervishes that spin
the red thread of all sorrows
into silver sheets of rain.

In the steady prayer of rain
you become an ecstatic dance
on the face of water.
In the deep memory of trees
you are the delight
of a caressing melody.

II.

THE PAST IS NOT DEAD

Shades of the prison house
Begin to close
Upon the growing boy…
It is not as it was of yore.
Turn wheresoever I may
By night or day
The light which I had seen I can now see no more.

—William Wordsworth

Father! Father! Where are you going?
O do not walk so fast.
Speak Father, speak to your little boy,
Or else I shall be lost.
The night was dark, no Father was there;
The child was wet with dew;
The mire was deep and the child did weep,
And away the vapours flew.

—William Blake
(from *Songs of Innocence*, "Little Boy Lost")

You Threw Me Down

-1-

You threw me down the stairs.
  My body launched backwards,
    initiated into the gravity of being BAD,
      evacuated like a product of waste,
        no longer useful,
          poorly made,
            circling down a drain.

I tumbled through space,
  scraping the air for something to hold,
    watching the Father's eyes inflame,
      seething with scowling contempt,
        as I fell farther into shame
          and excoriation.

All lights went out.
  I fell through a treacherous wind tunnel,
    slammed into silence
      at the bottom of the stairs
        sharpened like the teeth of a chainsaw.

A dangerous repose,
faraway sleep,
contortion of shadows,
smoldering in a pool of dense smoke,
a tar pit for creatures
close to extinction.
My wounded body,
heavy with twisted bones
and a pounding skull
could not rise up from the horror,
or slip out the door
dangling at a broken angle.
I lay awake through the paralysis of night
torn between
a desire to live
and a deepening distrust of life,
impotent tears,
tongue silenced,
mutilated down to the root,
collapsed like a corpse in the mouth's tomb
like the arms of a squid
unable to stir in the dim cave,
bitter clouds of ink,
stain of shame.

-2-

A long time passed.
All light faded and no one came,
no one witnessed

the pool of wounded light at dawn,
the gradual rising of the child body.
He picked himself up,
licked his blood like an animal.
Unaware of where he was
he began to move as faraway as possible
from the Father who put down uprising
with soul murder.

-3-

I moved on, hiding my wounds,
trying my best to become a man,
not knowing how to get it right,
dragging behind me a body without light.

For years I kept my distance.
But as my mother moved closer to death
I visited the family home,
shrinking as I entered.
The shadow at the bottom of the stairs
lived there,
everyone walked around it
or stepped over
the inconvenient corpse,
the family forgot to bury
and gave away his grave.

-4-

After 50 years I am standing next to him.
I am a shadow man,
he is old and shattered.
My mother has just died.
Father has lost his appetite for living.
A mysterious light pulsates
from the bottom of the stairs.
The humid August air
hangs over us, our fate,
despair of decades,
bitterness and smoldering grief.
He can barely speak.
Loss of his wife stretches his mind
beyond what he can endure.
Days go on endlessly,
no one is there,
no one to hear him
no one cares when he moans.
His words are broken.
He sobs like a motherless child…
"I feel so lost I don't know who I am anymore."
I hide my bitter smile, my sick pleasure,
the father cries out like a boy
who has been thrown out
of the safe and meaningful world
and I have no inclination to comfort him.

-5-

As I reach for the door to leave
it opens on its own, a familiar spirit entering the house.
I wince, noticing how the door hangs crooked
from an impact long ago.
Now where there was once horror
there is an open doorway,
a sweet summer breeze,
smooth ventilation of space,
a place to stand.
I am mysteriously drawn
to my father's woundedness.
We are both orphans,
always hungry, always unfed.
I can see in my father's eyes
that he wants to die,
know that soon he will have his way,
return to his provinces of absence.
But for this one precious moment,
he is standing here
at the opening door,
at the bottom of the stairs.
I am ready to leave him for the last time,
yet watching him like an eager child
to show me something.
I see his eyes tracing the shadow
lying there at our feet,
an interrupted life form

lingering for us to review.
For the first time ever
he reaches to embrace me.
In that rare holding
I feel a tiny hand reaching up for mine…
the child shadow rising to his feet,
joining us in this mystery of the expanding heart
where wounding and healing transcend time.
Outside the ancestors are gathering
to prepare him for the journey.
I too must travel far to find my home.
Once beaten to nothing,
broken tongue,
fear of love,
now I have found my voice
of imagination, of emotion,
instinct and story,
where woundedness lives
with despair and hope,
love and imperfection.
I am fractured and whole,
no longer living separate from life
but illuminated by it.

Remains

I knew you wanted to be dead.
You wanted to follow your wife
but that way would not open.
She did not last into the warm spring.
I buried my mother
but father, you would have nothing to do
with her cold body and casket,
the riot in the heart,
the tear in the ground
where she disappeared.
You left it up to me
to touch her lips and
drop her into the deep.
You slipped like smoke into
the spaces she left behind.

You prayed to your God.
He gave your cold, starving body,
a smoldering sorrow
to wrap around your bones,
like animal skin.

You went down to the creek one last time
hoping to hear the soothing voices
of water over smooth stone.
But the creek had run dry,
its jagged stones rising up out of dry sand
reminded you of tombstones
and your empty bed.

Nothing changed.
Your shuffling footsteps no longer mattered.
Each doorway
framed the passage into a new devastation.
Drifting in and out of dreamtime,
following the scent of grief,
you turned the corner,
imagining Dottie waiting for you at the table,
bathing in the same
old-time creamy light,
rising clouds of coffee and cigarettes.
In the harrowing realization
of her absence
God swallowed you,
spit you out, denied you,
proclaimed, "I will not have you yet,"
dropped you smoldering in Dottie's ashtray.

You retreated from the bleak rooms
where the haunting smell of cigarettes hovered.
You sat in one place
in a sunken hollow,
touched by nothing
and you read.
You heard voices.
Towering columns of sorrow
crept up and down the stairs.
The house began to give up its secrets.
And you read.
Your lampshade began to smolder,
the white on the pages began to lift up,
the white of your bones ached for burial.

The snow fell, everything white disappeared.
The windows streaked with ice
but there was nothing to see anyway.
I came and fed you like a child.
Dottie did not come.
God hid somewhere out in the woods.
The train stopped running down the track.
God called you from a distant station,
a mournful whistle,
from the end of the line.

When spring came,
you dreamed of swimming away.
For three days streaks of light fell,
swelling the creek,
beyond what it could endure,
until it jumped the banks,
rose up to your house
and took you.

I woke suddenly from a deep sleep,
heard a great clanging of steel,
a train thrusting forward,
its powerful engine shook the mountain
as it carried you away.

BLACK SNAKE

*We need books to affect us like a disaster, that grieve us
deeply…like being banished into forests far from everyone, like
a suicide. A book must be the axe for the frozen sea inside us.*

—Franz Kafka

HE took pleasure in blocking my light.
I was beaten back and broken,
a shadow cast away,
splattered like mold
in the dampening dim.
I retreated to hidden places,
cornered, humiliated,
something poorly made,
oozing to the floor,
dark matter, decomposing.

I devolved
into something misshapen,
a mutation of shame,
familiar with the stain of hate.

In the stillness of night
I felt myself becoming something unholy.
A disfigurement inhabited me,
the twitching and trembling of another creature
grew beneath my skin.

I carried my disease with me
like a suitcase heavy with demons,
a chorus of curses,
contemptuous voices inside my skull.
I grew to hate myself and
HIM inside me.

I hovered at the edge of extinction,
self loathing claimed me
with demonic force,
twisted my impotent shame into
a glorious beast of seething hatred,
hungry for annihilation,
cruel execution.

I began to take instruction
from the commotion of the stars,
whispering unimaginable atrocities.
They told me to wait
until the full moon
hung like a corpse.

Night came,
all light thinned to nothing.
The full moon rose,
a smear of ink,
tar rag nailed to the void,
my soul infected with evil.

Ascending the stairs in silence,
no light to guide me,
only the urgency of blood,
I found HIM sleeping.
I plunged my blade into HIS throat
so violently,
HE had but one moment
to honor HIS SON.
I cut the artery to end all words,
studied closely the formation of horror
taking shape in the mirror of his eyes,
HIS life gushing out
like water from a hose.

HE convulsed but could not cry out.
I quieted HIM,
decapitated HIM,
carried away HIS severed head,
hanging like a shattered lantern.

Slowly I left the awful quiet of that house,
a black snake slithering from
a rocky hole,
liberated and coiled,
licking the air
for the delicate scent of prey…
cruel kiss,
fierce blade,
ready to strike,

out into the merciless, unrelenting
pounding of night.

HIS head on top of mine,
my skull clammy with the Father's Blood,
I crawled beneath the largest tree.
The moon a swollen red wound,
shadows gathered like howling wolves,
serpents fell from twisted branches
of the tall oak
like stinging rain.
I IIS long thin shadow
slithered up my pants leg and up my shirt,
squeezed around my throat
like a warrior's necklace
or a shackle.
A haunting wind
mixed its broken body
with the ashes of the dead,
shrieked and wailed,
the headless Father
emerging from the house,
coming my way.

Fragmentation and Wholeness

Fragmentation prepares the path to wholeness, the mother of all origins and realization.

—Tao Te Ching

O Nobly born, O you of glorious origins, remember your radiant true nature, the essence of mind. Trust it. Return to it. It is Home.

—Tibetan Book of the Dead

Father, I was just a hungry child
longing to stand in your light.
You took me for an adventure
into the clear summer night
to behold the mystery
of stars and galaxies
burning in the infinite deep,
the brilliant fires of God's body.
Beneath the roar of those pulsating diamonds
my little candle body
flickered and leapt about
in the shadows at your feet.
You raised your arm
muscular and powerful
in a sweeping arc across the heavens,
as if you owned all the shimmering,

all the dark infinity.
With the noble proclamation of a king,
you traced a cluster of sparkling pearls
and named it Big Dipper.
I drew closer
with my empty spoon.
Leaning forward, face beaming
with the hope of being seen,
eager to learn your astronomy,
the calculus of getting near you.

I gazed up into the wonderment.
In the white dazzle of God's face,
I lost my bearings.
My mind spun like a compass
drunk on the wild magnetics of amazement.
When I turned to you with so many questions,
you had already slipped away
into your comfortable folds of dark space.
I saw the traces of you,
drifting formations of cloud,
trails of a smoky cigarette,
mixing with the milky river
of the galaxies.
You left me in bewildering emptiness
with my spoonful of shadows.

I was a hungry child searching
for an illuminated object,

traveling in a lonely orbit,
praying for one glimpse of you.
You wandered
in your vast elliptical patterns,
undetectable.
I searched with my telescope
like Galileo
deeper than all horizons
until I found Europa, moonchild of planet Jupiter
supreme god of all heavens
—400 million miles away.

Exhuberant, I ran toward you
like a firefly flashing its sheer radiance
—all it could ignite,
a trembling light beaming
in the anticipation
of being seen,
one chance to spotlight my achievement,
bask in precious mirrored light,
the proud father well pleased with his son.
My heart opened
like the wings of a soaring eagle
confident in the expectation
of acknowledgement.
I kneeled
with the certainty of my destiny as your prince,
awaited the royal sacrament,
the honor and the glory of your sword upon my shoulder.

You did not come.
You gave me nothing.
Your absence skewered me
down through the spine.

When I rose from my knees
the air was cold and the sky was empty.
I choked on something dying in me,
something inside
giving up on itself
because it could no longer be sustained,
like the fragile bird
that can no longer fly or be something useful
after crashing into its dream in the window.

The throne was empty.
I was a hungry ghost
longing to feed on the glory
of your reflected light,
left holding a spoonful of empty calories,
the sinking vapors of a useless dream.
You didn't see me,
I lost sight of you,
there was nothing left of you;
Emperor of absence,
you gave me
bewildering space,
the commotion of stars
clanging like spoons

in an empty bowl of sky
swirling down a hissing drain
pulling everything made of light
into oblivion.

Sometimes a young mind
is so impacted by the eclipse
of a dark shadow
it no longer maintains mastery of its own light.
Instead of revolving in its own elegant trajectory
the young mind drops,
behind everything,
falls beyond attachment and holding.
There is no comfort for the ghost that
roams in this cold colorless light.
An object that falls at the speed of darkness
into terrifying spaces
is known as a
particle of waste,
orphan litter,
bastard of absence,
leeching out into debris fields,
chilling distances of endless winter,
bones freezing at the marrow,
the body slowly cracks,
splits open like a piece of wood.

For decades I drifted beyond everything.
Out where all light thins to nothing,
night smolders with failing stars
choking on their own essential radiance,
eyes like white coals
staring with cold indifference.
Past the stars
there is no trace of raining light,
no flame survives
the vast dark waters.
I begged the Angels
in their ancient places
to take my life,
but they would only take my skin.
I eroded like a shapeless heap,
my face wore off,
my breath amounted to nothing.
The Angels took back my name,
glared with disdain,
turned their backs in disgust
at the odor of my shame.
Out on the edge of nothing
where the inchoate wind begins,
coiling itself like a serpent,
composing its voice
from the shrieks and screams
of lost souls,
their tattered skins clattering,

thrust through the absences,
all that is forsaken
is blown farther away.

Out there
the universe has its beginning
and its end.
Silent and still like a black orchid,
eyes gleaming white,
the Spider hovers on the rim of its black hole.
I was hung there,
the chains of Her design split me open.
I was taken into Her intimate sleep,
immersed in deepening brokenness,
impaled in Her hanging tomb for resurrection,
woven in Her shroud of integration,
the possibility of Being.
Deep in her body
She composed for me
the thin symphony of my Death song.

At the quiet limit of all worlds
I ended in Her silence
many universes deep.
She unbound me,
gave me the thread to find my way back
to my essence.
I was dying to live again

through the creation that
begins with ending
and ends with new beginning.
She held me
and there was nothing but holding.
I found new dimensions
in the communion of warm darkness.
I found a new face where
there was no time and no space.
I was nothing but letting go and being held
in infinite softness.
I became a strand of night pearls glowing,
a new heavenly formation
inspired by the loom of the Secret Mother,
my new name written among the constellations.
I breathed in the radiance
of darkness breaking into dawn,
breathed out into the threads of Her luminous web,
I breathed in and incarnated a new arrangement of life
into my body,
breathed out into the pregnant emptiness.

Tonight the sky is a black velvet dome,
glittering tapestry of ancient fires,
expansive prayer of vulnerability and longing,
revelation of the Outpouring Love that Loves us.
My young daughter and son have located the Big Dipper.
I proclaim that when the ladle tips,

brilliant new galaxies come pouring out across the heavens.
I tell them I am the poet of light, born in pregnant darkness,
child of the Secret Mother
who opens her cupped hands
to release her perpetual light.
Stars and galaxies stream through her fingers like jewels.
I extend my arm to locate
our names written in flames
across the face of God…
Caitlin, Ian, Ciarán.
We are that fire,
made of that Outpouring Love that Loves us.

III.
SHADOWS

Are there relations of the heart
that embrace what is most cruel
for the sake of wholeness?
For the world is only world
when everything is included.

—Rainer Maria Rilke

Always remember that when
the shadows within ourselves are touched
by the light of awareness
they become doors through which
Grace transforms our lives.

—Russ Hudson, The Ennegram Institute

How To Release a Shadow

-1-

The day ends.
There is a jagged tear in the sky
where day and night bleed into each other,
swirling colors of wounded light.
The remains
spread out like the precious sea glass
that glistens at the ocean's edge,
the undulating sea grass
spreading its thick curls
in the surge and the dragging away,
the immense rattling chains of the waves.

The sun casts off
its last light.
The luminous dark body of a tree
flares out its elaborate tentacles,
projecting a mysterious and terrible double.
You stand there
undead,
in the lengthening shadow,
a shade among the gathering ashes.

I stand, your obedient son
in the darkness that
long ago claimed me.

You stand beside the tree,
glare at me from your distance,
study my movement,
reach into my mind with a psychic hook.
You do not move,
you are dead
but you cannot rest.
I am your living flesh,
you need me.
I am seized by the fear of you,
the glare of a stalking predator,
a spider and its soul tomb.
I am defenseless as you wrap me in your shroud of shame.

You arise
whenever you want,
move through time outside of time,
rattling your chains,
an ancient howl inside my head.

I do not own my voice.
You buried my tongue,
silenced me.
You infiltrate.
An unholy entity
invades my psychic space,
inhabits the interior rooms
with mocking demons,
marionettes cursing as they gyrate on strings,

dangling from the walls.
I am occupied by alien voices,
colonized,
like a dark continent.

-2-

In the twilight between worlds,
when night incites dark armies of clouds
to push back the sun,
I rise up.
I go to your grave beneath the tree,
dig you up,
lift you gently from your box,
detach your skull,
raise it so that
we are eye to eye.
I gaze into your vacant stare,
witness in a flash
your birth, your life, your dying.
Deep inside the sockets
I see how your world
spun wildly,
beyond your control.
You stopped…
walked out on me…
abandoned your unlived life,
left it to me.

In the deepest formations of mind

behind your eyes,
I discover
a vast frozen lake of tears,
barren fields and a patchwork of stone walls,
a cathedral of sorrowing names,
cairns piled high for the ancestors of dreadful bleeding,
blades of the Chieftains flashing bright red,
bodies of warriors scattered like stones
in ghastly piles in the glistening rain.
For countless lifetimes we have been in battle,
we have murdered, been slain
by each other.
The voices in my blood tell me
I am made of grief,
betrayal and vengeance.
You are the Celtic Chieftain
who engineered the theatre of twisted bodies,
dying on the plains,
to serve your bloodlust and power.
I am the Prince who severed your head,
paraded it on the top of my spear.
May god forgive us both
our sins.

In the cosmos of god charged particles,
we are the exuberant diversity of elements,
we are the ambivalent forces,
formed in opposition,
born to collide,

the negative tension of chaos,
bloody sword of upheaval.

-3-

I kneel down beside you,
name my sorrows like constellations,
give voice to my tears as they release like rain,
splash upon your face,
fall through your mind's
deep canyons.
These tears ripple like waves
upon the shores of your abandoned provinces,
where compassion never reached,
warm light never arrived,
the recesses of barren ravines,
bone dry river beds.

This place of misery
is made sacred.
My tears soothe your wounds never touched by love,
shame mixing with winedark sorrow.
I tilt your skull to my lips,
drink deeply,
initiating a new consciousness.

-4-

With the knife of a warrior
I cut deep into my flesh,
extracting the two spikes you drove into my wrists,

the two manacles you hooked into the cage of my ribs,
the fastened chains
that bound your shadow to me
because I was born your son.
This inheritance I return to you.
This shroud is not mine to carry.

I spread your bones
on the quilt of your shadow,
this patchwork of wounds and shame.
Your bones glow from within.
The rays of dawn,
golden filaments of light,
untie the fixated cords we held so tightly,
binding us to each other's grief.
I release you softly back into the secrets of the earth,
where a sheltering darkness wraps
its wings around you,
offering you final rest.

-5-

This mysterious life
finally frees me
to forgive,
to love and live as your son.
I did not know I loved you,
I did not know you at all.

In the east
swirling waves of indigo and rose
rise up
like resurrected bodies of flame.
With this fire in my mind
I turn toward home,
walking in my own embodied light.

IV.
Awakening

Nature is a temple whose living columns
Co-mingling voices
Emerge at times.
Here man wanders through forests of symbols
Which seem to observe him with familiar eyes.

—Charles Baudelaire

O hear the voice of the Bard
Who present, past and future sees,
Whose ears have heard the holy Word
That walked among the ancient trees.

—William Blake (from *Songs of Experience*)

The Mind That Shapes the Flame

I dreamed that I stood in a large empty building with my father. He is elderly and I am middle aged. The walls are a brilliant white as are the towering cathedral ceilings. High above us a light is swinging wildly from a long chain. The light no longer works so I set up an enormous step ladder to change the bulb. As I begin to mount the ladder and I feel it sway beneath me, my father holds and stabilizes the ladder. I climb to the highest rung. Both the ladder and the light fixture are swaying and I can just barely reach the fixture as it swings toward me. With great concentration and precision I manage to insert a large new bulb into its metal channel and spin it until it makes connection. The entire room is shimmering white as I look down to see my father smiling up at me.

-1-

Last night
a great white dream.
You stood beside my bed
in shimmering folds of white light.
I was joyous when you took me by the hand.
You were my young father
and I was your boy.
You lead me back to a blessed time
long before the fall
and the sorrows
of the father, son and unholy ghost.

-2-

It is thoroughly winter.
My little legs sink deep in the fluffy snow.
It is 1961 and winter owns the landscape.
I am 6 years old.
We have left mother at home beside the warm hearth.
It is my time to explore beyond her shelter.
You have bundled me up
and prepared me for the initiation into
the forest of supernatural white.

You create a path for me to follow
through the tumbling and drifting mountains of snow.
We pass by the graves of ancient warrior kings, slumbering giants,
witch mounds, enchanted doorways into hidden worlds.
Snow falls upon my face,
tickles for a moment,
as the small furnace of my body
melts the delicate crystal.
I am your devoted disciple.
I follow in your footsteps.
Like a white god
you have gathered a snow capped mountain on your shoulders.
Avalanches tumble behind you,
white stars live and die at your feet.
We climb a hill and descend into a glen,
cross a bridge over a rushing stream.
The bridge has no railings.
I stumble when gaps in the planks reveal

an open throat below,
a churning white cauldron
frothing with snakes,
what I hear in the water's dizzying roar
wants me to fall.

When you stretch out your hand,
my mind steadies with a sudden courage,
my body stirs with fierce aliveness,
my strides are sure and balanced
guided by a streaming light
emanating from your heart.

-3-

You clear a sacred circle to reveal
the brown frozen earth.
We build a temple of dry wood.
Fire sparks from your fingertips.
The rising body of fire
twists and crackles
leaps and seizes
everything in its talons.
You fan the flames with our open palms.
I shape the flames with my mind.
My mind moves and
the fire whirls into wondrous forms;
the dark bear sleeping in its winter cave,
wolves howling in fierce red light,
rivers tumbling through gold canyons

emptying into vast green oceans,
the spirits of trees leaping from their charred bodies,
a gleaming scarlet god in the center of it all
outpouring new life.
Clouds spiral upward
forming a stairway between heaven and earth.

You melt snow in a metal pot.
I witness the miracle of a white body
turned into clear living water.
Your knife sharpens the tip of a stick.
Soon bread has been transformed into toast
for communion with hot tea.
A third cup of tea and toast
is placed beneath a tree,
an offering for the ancestors.
In the cathedral of the still white forest,
we listen closely to their gradual arrival…
steady murmur of sky snow,
intimacy of wind,
voices of water,
memories of trees,
body prayer of crackling fire.

I stand closer to the braids of flame
and I feel woven into you.
I am your son with whom
you are well pleased.
You are the loving mind of these trees,
the living spirit that has blessed my mind with flame.

I am the living flame that grows
in the power and glory of your shadow.

-4-

The weather changes.
The snow falls wildly,
like streaming white ribbons.
I hear clouds shattering.
The forest is streaked with a dense film.
I watch the falling snow
spiral above the fire
the way shooting stars leave a sleek trail
as they drift, plunge, burn.
You are uneasy and agitated.
We leave the white bones hissing in the fire.

You are moving down the path.
I fear I will be left behind.
The snow stings.
I follow you to the bridge.
You are in a hurry to cross
where I cannot follow.
You turn back,
your eyes speak
about the mystery of love and fear.
You reach for me.
Like a burning crystal of snow,
pierced and cradled

in the open arms of a noble oak,
my little flame body is held.

When you turn away to make your crossing,
an expanding galaxy of light
tumbles from your shoulders,
white stars rise in swirling commotion,
everything begins to move away from everything else.

Belonging to This World

(for Jordan)

This boy with the mischief smile
and sky blue eyes
is my grandson, Jordan.
At age two I held a tiny garter snake in my hand
and introduced Jordan to one of god's little creatures.
He was not pleased by the long neck without arms or legs
or the gaping mouth and the slithering.
His face distorted with horror,
he burrowed deep in his father's arms and screamed.
So eager to please and be loved
but exposed as a fool,
I had to creep away with the legless serpent
like an illegitimate creature.

For one full year Jordan would not forgive me.
I approached with stuffed bears and terror seized him.
The toy trucks were shunned because my scent was on them.
At age three I presented him with a salamander
and prepared myself for the final banishment.
He squealed with delight and loved it immediately,
this baby dinosaur that stomped the smooth terrain of his palm
the way it's ancestors shook the new earth.

Today on his fourth birthday
I have given Jordan a turtle.
He is astonished to see a creature
carrying a home upon it's back.
They become fast friends.
Like Jordan, the turtle is not gifted with speed
but with steadfast determination,
stretching his neck forward and marching vigorously
across the lawn toward the forest,
eyes glowing with flames of imagination.
At the edge of the forest,
Jordan prevents an escape by lifting him up by his rooftop.
He squeals with delight at this
turtle swimming in the air,
dreaming of plunging into the deep pond of his ancestors.

The sun begins its descent toward the mountains
as we walk into the forest to turtle's home.
On the muddy shore we release our glorious friend.
He waddles and dives beneath the green skin of the pond,
disappearing into the murky depths
where he belongs.
As we turn toward home Jordan says,
"Papa, let me hold your hand".
My heart breaks open in a prism of light.
His hand in mine,
like a tiny leaf,
I am not sure if I am guiding Jordan
or he is leading me now

into a new dimension of the heart.
With each small step,
the voices of more birds.
The wisest of all,
the black crow,
calls out from the top of the noble white pine,
welcoming us
into the corridors of the forest.
This place of lengthening shadows,
slanting rays of sun,
columns of green flame,
is sacred ground.
The ancestors move between realms of light and space,
witnessing but never interfering,
patiently awaiting acknowledgement.

Jordan and I are holding hands.
The path is disappearing yet
we are finding our way.
The crow announces the shifting of space
as I feel a new hand joining ours.
My deceased father holds my tiny hand and guides me
through a cathedral of trees
to a place where I feel I belong,
where fireflies fill up the rooms of the forest,
sparkling like the eyes of the watchful ancestors.
Each flickering light is the new life that is ignited from the old,
a spiral thread woven through the generations.

In the diminishing light three people stand,
looking homeward,
surrounded and animated by timeless presence,
where everything is forgiven and released
into a continuous stream of birth and death and rebirth.
A candle flame passes from one body to the next
in a procession of light,
seeking its fullest incarnation.
This is where we take our place in the world,
lean into the mystery of this life that wishes
to enter through us,
to take root in this soil
that will yield equal harvests of love and fear.
This is the ground of being and
belonging to this world.

Dark Beauty

(In search of a muse)

-1-

The distances between us are so bewildering.
I can never possess you
although you possess me.
You live somewhere in my body
but I can never find you by seeking you.

Nothing seems to hold us together,
yet your dark beauty smolders in my imagination,
lingers on my tongue,
flares up with wounding light
when the body aches at night.

Although I cannot touch your skin
I can find you deep in the nightscape.
While my body sleeps without you
my soul delights in dreaming your secret shape
into a body of desire I can hold.

Among the towering columns of clouds,
piercing lightning,
I singe my wings on the brilliant fires,
sail the river of stars
through streams of luminous beings,

golden angelic ships
masts abundant with God's breath.

From high above the blue hills
I see you waiting at the gate.
I drift down into a lush meadow,
where you take me into
the mystery of dark brown eyes,
the radiant smile of the muse,
lips glowing wet,
flowing black curls of the sacred consort.
My kiss on your dark flesh,
sizzles in the moist rain
beading on your breasts.

You whisper into my lips,
"we are never separate."
You dream into me,
the wind joins us
swelling like the ocean-body,
flooding the meadow with golden-light,
bliss-drenching our one body.

Come closer now,
become a gentle rain tonite.
Let each water droplet on your skin
become a prayer bead for me to enter-
this rain…
your soft animal flesh…
and I…

will enter this stream
and dissolve,
until I no longer know if I am
a rain melody,
a streaming silver storm,
or a moist dream
sweeping through this meadow of stars.

-2-

The dawn light takes you.
You cannot be held for long.
Our flight is hopeless and beautiful.

The dangerous currents may pull my wings
down into the copper sea
or I may fly too high
past the incense of the stars,
beyond all holding,
and freeze in the black deep.

In these bewildering distances,
you offer only a dreamtrace
to linger on my tongue
as I fall.

My Beautiful Ruins

Yeshua said,
"I shall destroy this house
And no one will be able to rebuild it."

(from the Gospel of Thomas)

For what is the mind to do
with something that becomes the mind's ruin;
a God that consumes us
in His grace?

—Saint Catherine of Siena

The sky was cruel that night.
Darkness collided with the wind
and descended like a dragon,
talons slicing open the roof of my home,
tearing away my most cherished holdings.
I heard the howling of demons,
grinding commotion of stars,
terrible groaning of the fabric of reality
as it was torn,
ancient chains clattering,
wild gyration of god particles
as my house splintered and came undone.
I ran naked into the street,
rejoicing in liberation from all the false trappings
of this dazzling world.

The sweet melody of revolution was cascading
down through the collapsing frame of all that I own,
and the secret one was dancing on my rooftop,
leaping like a child,
whirling over the skeleton of twisted bones.

As the world melted away I welcomed the obliteration
and reserved a special place at my table
for the guest who delights in destruction.
I prepared tea beneath a transparent sky,
as the honey of the moon
began pouring itself
through the cracks above,
flooding and blessing
my beautiful ruins with light.

Soon all structure was gone.
Only my teapot remained,
overflowing with the moon's radiance.
All night my laughter echoed back to me
from the eroding mountains.
I became unhinged and unframed,
sipping the most precious moonlight from my teacup,
while the broken world fell away.

THE PALACE OF WIND AND LIGHT

(for the awakening of my German brother, Stefan)

Oh my friends, why do you sleep?
Why do you not search
the vast house of your heart?

—Hildegard von Bingen

-1-

In the high plateau of the Rhön mountains
the sky was sleeping in the meadow.
A gentle mountain breeze
embraced the mist
as they spread out over the tall grass.
Their moist bodies became an
expanding symphony,
high in the palace of wind and light.

Ciarán heard every tone and felt every texture
of this intricate melody.
The gods were blending dark sorrow with red dawn,
broken hearts with white flame,
the way Christ mixes the clay of earth
with the moist breath of resurrection,
liberates the blind from darkness,
turns the chains of the dead,
into open tombs.

-2-

The mountains rattled,
lurched from their foundations,
releasing a silver cascade of rivers
that flooded the meadow with a glistening ocean,
with the urgency of spirit
fulfilling a new incarnation.
The mountains roared
when Wotan and the gods descended
riding great white stallions,
pulling golden ploughs
that furrowed the sea.
In the precision between waves
rows of sun-drenched crops flared up,
swaying and swelling bodies,
fertile flames dancing,
in the space of water and sky
and no horizon.
Ciarán watched each flame body rise,
ripen in the bending sunlight,
then collapse as empty husks,
the way we all fall,
gently combed back into the clear light
by the hands of many gods,
fields tilled for the body to lie beneath,

long blue shadows swallowed by night,
flickering fire invited home into fiercer light.
As thunderously as they arrived
the gods retreated on shadow horses,
folding the groaning sea
back into rolling meadow.
When the sky was red gold
with the new dawn
Ciarán climbed out of his husk
and prepared his way
for a new incarnation in the Rhön .

-3-

In the palace of wind and light
Ciarán lives as fisherman do,
ambivalent regarding the hard earth
beneath his feet,
faithful to a deeper longing
to row toward god.
He leaves the shore far behind,
following a quiet calling out on the mist,
the way Peter stepped out of his boat
and was suddenly incarnated
into his own fullness,
called the way poets are,
to walk out on the foam of waves
to their own open fields.

When the new dawn casts out
its pearls of dazzle upon the waves,
Ciarán walks out upon the glittering carpet of flames,
drives away all demons of doubt
and fears of going under,
drops his fishing nets into the deep,
casting out his words,
prayers and unsinkable visions.
With the patience of a saint
he waits
for that deep inward pull
of underlying presence.
A terrible faceless beauty seizes him,
takes him down
into a luminous web,
the gentle swaying of awakened light.

The Poetry of Bending Light

(for Br. Don Bisson)

It is very much a human impulse to try to picture God
and God does come to find us in those very pictures,
as well as in the smashing of them.
Our inability to cross over the gap
between our pictures and God's reality
is met by the unbelievable miracle
of God crossing over to us.

—Ann Belford Ulanov

It is difficult to tell
when the eagle soars,
if it is spirit or flesh,
the contour of a soul,
a rising body of flame,
or an emanation of
the radiance deeply hidden.
These wings streaked with golden sun
trace a secret prayer
spiralling up through
the towering palace of white winds,
blue fire,
and the invisible light
behind all things.
Ciarán has studied this movement

since he was a child
shaping clouds with his mind.
He is old now
but he still finds a way
to sneak off in secret,
to drop to his knees,
roll over on his back to pray;
"Does this eagle have some design in mind
when she plunges in a swooping arc,
lifts, swirls and soars elegantly,
drawn like a magnet toward the floating furnace of the sun,
shrieking as she brushes against the velvet
of God's face?
Does she discern a clear path
within the rivers of vapors
streaming through the windfield?
Or does she abandon intention and determination altogether,
faithfully surrendering herself into unseen waves
of bending light?"

All of his life Ciarán has tried to fathom this mystery of joining;
How the tree leans to embrace the wind,
How a cloud is gracefully possessed by a greater force,
How God's breath becomes a sculpture within stainless space,
How the mystics see the flames that shape the Mind,
How all things change when Mind moves.

Now Ciarán is exhausted by thought.
He kneels down in pure experience.
His words take off in flight,
drawn by the deepening pull
of wings and oars rowing toward God,
snow white sailing ships
ascending into luminous blue,
glistening in the lips of the wind,
the inner radiance of space,
beyond knowing.

But it is not Ciarán
who shapes these flames of mind into poetry.
The mystic arc of the eagle
was written inside him
from the beginning.
The Secret One guides his hand,
strokes of bending light,
momentary glimpses of the eagle piercing the sun,
fragments of a memory
of God piercing his soul.

V.
LAMENTATION

The tremendous world I have inside my head,
But how to free myself
And free it
Without being torn to pieces?
I would a thousand times rather be torn to pieces
Than retain it in me or bury it.

—Franz Kafka (from his diaries)

V.
Lamentation

The tremendous world I have inside my head,
But how to free myself
And free it
Without being torn to pieces?
I would a thousand times rather be torn to pieces
Than retain it in me or bury it.

—Franz Kafka (from his diaries)

ELEGY FOR A DRUID PRIEST

(for Gerard Francis O'Rahilly)

-1-

Ciarán and the Talking Skull

I dreamed that you were taken from us
by the Dark Sorcerer
who fled down his dreadful hole
into the Otherworld,
held you captive in a ghost trance
of neither sleep nor waking,
prepared you for dismemberment.

I heard you calling out in terror,
followed your voice
through a Dark Wood
of disfigured forms.
I disappeared into a doorway
at the roots of a tree,
dropping into that spirit realm
where you had fallen.
My body tumbled
into the hot, damp stench of oblivion.
Time and space fractured
like ice that will not hold.
Down this dark shaft
I scraped against a cutting wall

of serrated spikes,
teeth and tongues of hissing demons
lashing out
from their fissures.

I found you
decapitated,
hanging from a barren tree—
no wind to carry you home,
no ground to gather your bones,
no standing stone to honor you.

I, Ciarán, sang a song of enchantment
to liberate you from the evil spell,
sorrows of your floating tomb.
I carried your severed head
like a lantern,
columns of light flaming
from your talking skull.
We crossed the Perilous Bridge
of knives and spears together,
rose out of the dark,
into new light.

Standing in the Sacred Center
of the Oaken Grove
I proclaimed…
"I, Ciarán, bring undying light
into the shapeless deep
where sorrow lives.

I am the Shimmering Dagger that severs
the Sorcerer's black cloak.
I am the Fearless One,
undeterred by the Sorcerer's Spell
or fires of Hell,
I retrieve stolen souls
from all hidden provinces.
I cross all dimensions,
shift into many shapes
to heal dark maladies of the soul.

I am the light
dazzling on the water's face.
I am the glowing foam of waves
high in the milky galaxy.
I am the dawn star
dissolving the curtains of night.
I am the roar of the ocean.
I am the eagle's shriek.
I am blood on the Dagger's edge.
I am the destroyer of chains,
the imagination of trees
walking about while men sleep.
I am the risen one."

-2-

The Ancestors
We were brothers,
born in County Galway, Ireland,

land of savage beauty,
precious green marble of Connemara,
transplanted in America
in grade school.
I felt lost and without a place in the new world.
Younger by one year and gracefully extroverted,
my brother fit right in with his Irish charm.
Troubled when I lost my Gaelic language
to the new dispensation of education and mind control,
I struggled to find my ground, my ancestors.
I was not lost for long.
The ancestors found me!

I had taken my brother deep into the forest.
He did not appreciate the unexplained movements
and murmurings of this unfamiliar province.
Even the wind had a different taste
than the breezes that came off the seas
onto our blessed Irish homeland.
He looked up to me as a brave explorer.
He was gifted with a bright light of intellect
but carried a strange bundle of fears.

I followed the sun-drenched fountains
of leaf-green light
that spilled off the canopy of trees,
illuminating our way.
We crossed the rushing stream of many voices,
our small legs churning against the mountain's powerful pull.

We rested on the massive boulders,
grey elephants and rhinoceros with bulging folds of skin.
The silver trout eyed us from his cool deep pool.
For me this landscape was alive with language and wisdom,
the living cycle embedded in me.
Gerard wanted to go home.

We feasted in a golden meadow, rich with blueberries.
Drunk on the juicy sweetness, my mind unclear,
I drifted off the path.
As twilight came upon us I rejoiced in the in-between colors
but my brother's eyes darted fitfully
at the shadows rustling about deeper in the dense woods.
I encouraged him that home was not far
but knew we were closer to a new threshold.

Beneath the mantle of nature
light thinned out and darkness hovered,
each moment opening to unseen reality.
I did not point out to my brother,
deeper into the shadows,
the animals shifting shapes,
trees walking,
the gigantic gnarly tree swaying
in the melody of the croaking frogs.

Exhausted in the dusk,
we ascended a hill,
but no way home appeared.
Confused, I lowered and gripped my head,

straining for a solution.
And then I heard by brother shout
"a light, a light, over there."
Down below a faint light
seemed to float in mid-air.
We ran as if we were on fire,
approaching close enough to see
a swinging lantern held by no one,
heading down the railroad tracks,
in the direction of a larger fire.

Following the light
we left the railroad tracks,
ascended a trail
up the side of a shale mountain,
found a fire burning under an overhang,
the pink flesh of roasted trout laid out for us.
Large stones sang as the flames warmed them,
but no one greeted us.
Soon our small bodies curled by the fire.
I told my brother about the great Thatcher-God
who roofs the sky with stars
so that children can sleep peacefully,
safely protected beneath the smooth dome of heaven.
The whole universe looked down upon our fire.
My heart rejoiced at my brother's smiling slumber.
I did not sleep because the ancestors had teachings for me
beside the fire that burns in all places in all times.
A train roared through the shale mountain

with a light larger than the moon.
I was sailing away on the rolling seas,
cradled in a sturdy boat,
all the way home to blessed Ireland.

After high school
we took our separate paths.
You assimilated into the American dream.
I watched with envy as you,
the scholar-athlete,
achieved your Ivy League entitlements,
ascended into your power.

You were the Golden Boy,
apprenticed at age twenty-two
to the wealthy suits of Wall Street,
elevated yourself rapidly
up the Manhattan Sky Towers
that pierced the sky,
revealing the good fortune
spread out before you.
I took my own path of
inward provinces,
riding the rails,
praying for a muse.
I patched together a wardrobe
of suitable personas,
cardboard cutouts,

inflatable masks
like an emergency roadside kit
for someone pretending
to be someone.

Spiritual Wasteland

You did not last
in the spiritual wasteland.
We celebrated your twenty fourth birthday in 1980.
You were slipping into madness.
We hiked to the shale mountain,
our sacred site,
where we had once found safety when lost.
Now we were young men crossing the frontier,
far from the foundation of childhood,
sinking in the shifting sands of adulthood,
reaching out for inspiration,
struggling for accomplishment,
something to believe in,
anything to celebrate.

Our innocence had once given us freedom
to lean into larger spaces
of our own becoming.
Now we examined ourselves and each other
for the wounds where we had been hammered
into confining shapes.
When I looked into your eyes,

I felt a raw instinctual terror,
saw the sobbing angels,
lost my breath,
pulled back
in disbelief.
The fire beside us stirred in erratic patterns.
You blurred out of focus,
seemed strange and unfamiliar,
as if some alien entity had infiltrated your brain,
occupied you and colonized you,
then emptied out your essence
like Imperialists who enslave the natives,
pillaging the mines of gold.
Your beautiful mind ravaged,
your voice rattling incoherence.
I watched helpless, haunted.
I had never seen someone disappear.
The pupils of your eyes,
wildly enlarged,
expanded like sky.
A jagged tear in that membrane
opened to reveal
a glaring, protruding eye,
a black hole with a piercing lens
that watched and watched.
The deepening skies of your eyes
grew fierce,
boiled slowly like storms clouds

expanding into infinitely white,
scalding light.

-4-

Chapel of the Original Flame

We sat high on the blue grey cliffs,
a silver freight train coming around the bend,
roaring, pounding...
thunder and smoke,
shaking the mountain from its roots,
rattling our teeth,
our eyes tearing with euphoria.
We watched the train pass far below
as we had so many times as children,
our young bodies trembling with new power,
sure aliveness,
minds swelling with leaping flames
and visions.

I imagined the Irish laborers,
more than one hundred years before,
forging this rail pass through a shale mountain,
laying down steel tracks,
their bodies heaving engines,
rising columns of steam.
In the roaring silence
when the train had passed,
I heard the echoing ping
of ghost hammers

driving spikes deep into wood.
Looking into your eyes
I saw fragments of mirror glass,
walls of your mind crashing,
opulence of your soul eclipsed-
a torn eyelid,
a blackened sun,
a floating tomb,
blighted fruit—
a dream that could not get off the ground.

Together, in silence
we followed the fading melancholy
of the whistle calling out for home.
It became a whisper absorbed into space,
like the wild geese
soaring through their sadness,
calling their lament.
I wondered
if we wander too far from home,
where no one remembers our name,
and despair grows too heavy
who will find us
who will remember our story?

In the tremendous quiet
we descended the precarious cliffs,
finding old familiar roots to grasp,
to stabilize our footing on the shale,
crumbling beneath our feet,

not quite anchored in
the impossible vertical world.
At the parallel tracks
we balanced lightly along the rails.
Placing a coin on the silver steel,
I imagined the next train derailing,
rising up gently
to escort us both safely away,
high over the mountain,
through the heart of the sun,
deeper into the monastery of the stars,
to the chapel of the original flame.

The sun was setting,
you, eerily preoccupied
by inner callings,
mocking and angry voices
twisting the corner of your mouth,
with abrupt contortions
as if wrestling with an angel,
lamed deep within.

Bold bleeding colors drained the sky.
A flaming wheel
embedded in foaming clouds,
projected the mystery of broken light
in spears of Christ Rays.

I prayed in this immensity,
that God would shelter you,

shatter you no further.
The trees heard my prayer,
followed us like a wave of compassion
across the mountainside.
Tall slender bodies,
heads bowed,
radiating sparks of light
along the ridge.
The forest walked,
mirrored our movement,
marched mournfully,
like a slow procession of clouds.

You balanced on the rail,
your sandals lightly touching
the silver tips of waves,
walking on water,
barely holding on.
I watched you tilt your head
as if hearing for the first time
the clear chime of a temple bell
calling you to step out of your world,
urging you to let go
of the fragile foundation you cherished,
to find the sure salvation
of an outstretched hand
there in the storm.
I watched you reach out,
palms skyward,

waiting for something certain
to hold
like an abiding faith
that Christ would raise you up,
never let you drown in your madness.

-5-

End Days

The tragedy began
in Manhattan,
the City without sleep,
haunted by the unbearable
multitude of lights,
dazzling glass,
surface flames,
smoke rising from the streets.
Heat lightning, flickering madness,
fallen angels with red shadows
prowling their unholy hungers.
In the city ablaze
with over-lit skies,
no protection for the mind,
no shield from the cosmic rays
assailing hallucinations.

Day and night he dreamed
a most convincing dream
that his face was all used up.
So, a second face grew

on the back of his skull,
a face that evolved
to shield him
from the devouring world.

He took his new face with him
to the Macy's Thanksgiving Day Parade,
inflated with confidence
in his new adaptation.

The red dawn released
a multitude of perfumed clouds
that lingered over Manhattan
as if blessing the launch
of this festival of mind—
the fluid harmony of marching bodies
the precision of drum, horn, and magic wands.

Spirit pours out the depths of its potentiality,
fantasies have wings that fly down the avenue—
fleets of noble sailing ships,
masts abundant with colorful winds,
white swans floating like heavenly bodies.
soaring through the canyons of skyscrapers.
Clowns set free their magic balloons,
a carnival of leaping animals morphing in mid-air.

Gerard marched with a Cheshire Cat grin,
amused by the laughter arising in his skull.

The rhythmic drums like a soothing heartbeat,
the swirling, twirling dancers
with long, shapely legs
become his beautiful lovelies,
beckoning him to follow.
His body merges with the marching band
down the avenue of towering steel.

Like warriors on the killing field
the clouds are ambushed and dismembered—
the sky turns inside out
an infinitely pale haze
full of trembling possibilities
of reverie or atrocity.

The inside is out and the outside is in.
Thoughts float free without a thinker,
feelings are streaks of color without an owner,
appearances look for a body to inhabit.
Blue-sky crayon smears inside the skull,
dripping white words on the horizon,
red shadows sliding off surfaces,
staggering in the street.
A twirling baton becomes a Ferris wheel,
tumbling umbrella of cosmic light
crashing into the crowd.
A White Beast passes over the sun,
an immeasurable pounding beats
within the blazing furnace of the skull.

Whiplash panic.
The sky grinds sideways,
flashes bone-white fangs.
Light spears strike the streets of Manhattan.
The back of the wind is a menacing white howl.
Lucifer descends like a dragon
from the dark side of the sun,
bolts of white flames flare from his wings.
Lucifer parades his stolen light down Broadway.
Master of Ceremonies,
Prince of Atrocities,
his flaming torch
a bouquet of writhing serpents.
The marching band is a staggering mass of skeletons,
a dirge of clacking bones,
melting flesh.
Lucifer whips the melancholy clown
carrying his eyes in a bowl of tears.
John the Baptist drags his head behind him
on a chain.
Christ has mostly disappeared
down the deep throat of the hooded cobra,
his stubborn wooden cross is all that saves him
from the long slithering chasm into
the belly of the serpent.
Majestic balloons are no longer tethered,
drifting away with smoldering bodies,
dangling dark spiders on silken sky thread.

A murder of crows descends
upon the children.
Lucifer melts all structure, material and substance
into a tide of white fangs.
Even the gods turn their backs and flee this wasteland.
The sky inverts itself with a jolt.
The edgeless, screaming white light
enters Gerard thoroughly,
lives beneath his skin,
inside his bones.
Nothing exists outside that skin,
Nothing is real outside the mind,
the mind and skin extend everywhere.
A Glaring Eye sees all.

Gerard takes the last northbound train,
a streaming silver crypt,
hurtling out of Grand Central to Poughkeepsie.
Behind him the fury of the skyline,
Manhattan burning like a funeral pyre.
Turning away,
turning inward,
he slumps over in his seat,
slides down into the deepening chasm of himself.
On his right,
the claws of the sun
thrash the treetops,
glare into his window.
On his left

a bay of ghouls,
the tides of the Hudson River
have turned upstream,
black waves like the hoods
and fangs of cobras
strike at his window,
flooding the tracks.
The air roars as everything burns.
The train screeches,
tilting too far off
the melting silver rails,
plunges into the flaming river
and sinks.

No longer trapped in a drowning machine
but now inside the belly of a Powerful Silver Salmon,
diving deep beneath all terror
into a sheltering darkness,
hidden in silence,
mind emptied of predators,
wild river emptied of its thrashing,
riding the quiet currents home.

-6-

Lord of Gentle Currents

Delivered safely by the Salmon
to a smooth bed of grass
beside a familiar stream,
he slept for days,

woke up to psychic convulsions,
forgetting how to breathe the air
or put his mind together.
He crawled like a creature
to the doorstep of his childhood home,
but found no consolation in these rooms.
Devouring light still blazed
in the furnace of his skull,
dark malady deconstructing him slowly.
Lampshades smoldered
while the Glaring Eye kept watch.
Walls roamed about at night,
grew eyes that migrated across the ceilings.
While Gerard slept
his bed floated like a white sailing ship,
out through the channels of a widening sea,
the smooth ventilating space of silken waters.
But each night a storm arose
from beneath the waves
took him down the deep throat of the sea
swallowed him deeper still.

Abandoning this world,
he found consolation in his shamanic hut
beside the stream,
with no lights on,
no one to answer the door,
hidden like a wild animal,
forgetful of himself,

his kinship with others.
In the forest
he built a shrine to Mary,
Blessed Mother of All Sorrows.
At night
he curled his body like a child
at the feet of the Mother of Mercy
who cries the tears of those who suffer alone.
In the warm darkness
he slept in peace
as she wept into his wounds,
silenced the demons
that riot at night.

Farther into the wild
he slipped out of his cursed humanity,
waded into a deepening mountain stream,
transformed his body
into the long, smooth muscle
of the Noble Rainbow Trout.

In the Kingdom of the Quiet Underworld
he dwelled in a floating palace,
Lord of Gentle Currents,
embraced by the infinite softness
of water's soothing hands.
He opened his new gills to receive
the Breath of God,
incorporated the pure Living Water.
He slept in the timeless stream

beneath a cool sheltering sky,
the shimmering mosaic of the sun's face,
sparkling rippling light,
transparent all the way to God.

-7-

Unsayable Misery

In this brief life
your flame went wilder and higher,
deeper into the chasm of you,
where heaven and hell,
deities and demons,
live and die in a cauldron of storm.
Now, my soul brother,
you lie in a bed of stillnesss.
In this ritual of grieving
we have lifted you up,
placed you in your sleeping box
of satin and oak
so we can face
what is dead in you.

The men kneel before you,
quietly slip into the darker room,
drink deeply of the merciful Irish whiskey,
each measured prayer
choking back the grief
of those who do not wish to feel the real.

The women
huddle in whispers,
agree that God is good,
say a prayer
that there will be no schizophrenia in heaven,
your earthly curse of madness will die in the grave,
your new wings will instantly carry you beyond your torment.

I kneel at the open casket,
begin to move among
the living parts
left in you,
your eyes alive with psychic storm
rising from what is most ancient and undying.
Something flares out from beneath
your shuttered eyelids,
pulsing waves of demons and gods,
like a swarm of bats
fleeing the throat of their cave.

The mourners who still linger
feel a sudden uneasiness,
an urgency to flee
the vague shadows
contorting in haunting lamentation
on the walls,
because tonight
outstretched arms
from the spirit world

will reach out
into the living space of the parlor,
like the forms of dark enchantment
that seek us in our dreams at night.

Tonight, my brother
as you transition between worlds,
the furnace of your mind
will burn into a conflagration
of visions exiting your body,
hallucinations of primal terrors.
Everything you have feared and hated and denied
will crash like mirrors,
reflecting back to you
how you have lived and died repeatedly,
your structure stripped bare
and formed again in a new dispensation.

Your outer breath does not move
but the inner breath still abides.
I will kneel with you into the long night
and join your breathing.
You are without horizon or center
but brother, I am here now to call out your name
as you dissolve like salt into sea,
as your awareness burns like candle into boundless light,
as your soul expands into infinite transparency.

I will stand in my own embodied flame,
interpret the fire in my own head.

Voices in my blood tell me
I must remember your story.
I am the memory-keeper,
the witness bearer.
I try to give shape to my bewilderment,
unshakable awe.
Why did this bewitchment enter you
but pass over me?
You lost the struggle for your mind;
I am at a loss for coherent meaning.
But, I will use these inadequate words
to honor your nobility and madness,
how you lived your affliction with bravery.

Perhaps I will never comprehend
your transformation
but I will always hold the mystery of you,
even as my poem smolders at the corners,
curls into smoke,
imagines itself into ash.

In this life I have been taken to the rim of the heart
where sorrow hangs in silence from a leaning tree
and is not consoled.
This may be a haunting place full of empty space
or a doorway into stillness beyond our imagining
where words flee from each other,
everything comes apart,
everything begins to rapidly move away

from everything else,
where we become infinitely strange to ourselves,
so removed from the source
of what is knowable.

The church fills with the incense of the stars,
the fear of what lies beyond.
The casket sways like a rocking cradle
because we are all children afraid of the dark.
Colored light from the stained glass
ignites the hazy smoke rising toward the crucifixion,
casting a golden shadow
where Gerard hangs
between the crosses of cancer and madness.
We carry his body from the church,
stare into the hole that will be his home,
the exit wound from this transit to the next.

A penetrating light from over the ridge breaks
through the latticework of this world,
with a mosaic of shifting shapes
flashing images of a time when we were young brothers.
Standing high on the cliffs,
his silhouette,
saturated in light,
handsome, strong, confident—
bright emerald eyes flashing with possibilities of becoming.
Suddenly his eyes blaze with terror and go dim,

the smoky white light of hell
envelops his body,
steals the personality away,
leaving the rind of a strange fruit.
The outer world shrinks away from him,
his interior expanding beyond comprehension,
his mind lurching in the void.
Who he was, disperses
leaving only an incoherent shell,
a precious mind hollowed out,
a soul stolen away to the haunted dominion.
An unsayable Misery Beyond Commiseration.
He dies repeatedly,
melting in God's furnace,
until he is gone,
but lives on as someone else.

-8-

Minds Glow with Fire

I climb the blue grey cliffs one last time.
The silver train tracks are no longer there,
but now a ribbon of blue river
winding through a valley of stone.
Far above, the wild geese are flying into the west…
away from here… away from here
they soar,
their bodies glowing
as they bark their grieving melody.

Their lament mixes with a rhythm far below,
of ancient hammers against metal.
On the river's shore, I see heaving painted bodies,
long wild hair, muscles rippling.
Celtic warriors sharpen their long, narrow swords;
flames leaping from their silver blades.
Minds glow with fire,
a Druid priest waves his arms in wild wizardry,
feverish incantation,
calling out to the God Lugh
to bring back the fading light,
chase away the gathering Black Ravens.
His words, once as powerful as a Thunder Hammer,
now fall like dying leaves in the roaring winds
of the angel's wings,
the sheltering folds that gather the light of his story,
lift his soul away.

-9-

The White Heat of Your Soul

The Druid priest has died.
At twilight we lay his body in a coracle,
send him out upon the River Shannon.
Warriors fill his boat with arrows of fire.
He drifts by and by,
into the Great Open Sea.
Long into the night,
the Druid's embers dance on the water.

I, Ciarán the Bard, stand watch and sing his elegy,
guard the blaze that he cast upon the world.
I bear witness to
this purest light that interweaves all dimensions,
passes like a candle flame,
from one precious incarnation to the next.

Farewell my ancient Druid friend,
you of noble ancestry,
you who have forgotten who you are,
lost all trace of your story, your priesthood,
wandered too far,
burning your mind on the rim of the otherworld.

I, Ciarán, will bear witness to your story,
just as Taliesin the Bard enchanted the court of Arthur
and extolled the magic of the Druid Merlin,
I will keep your spirit alive with poem and wind and fire,
bring your dreaming back to your homeland.
Look for the spiraling smoke
that rises like a soul ladder
for the spirits to cross over
and come near.
In this space I make sacred for you,
soul doors open,
the veil between the worlds is
as thin as a hair,
salvation as delicate as twilight,

suffering as empty as wind.
The flames of my mind
whirl the fire into different shapes…
brokenness and healing
unfold and braid together as one.

A hanging lantern shakes in the wind,
shadows splinters into light..
I feel the white heat of your soul come near.
The ancestors join us beside the fire of belonging,
swaying flames, dissolving sorrows,
Saints and Druids sing their ancient poems of enchantment
uniting our minds like braids of bending light,
until only the fire remains.

VI.
LOVING VESSEL

*....you want to live and you
want to love and you will
walk across any territory
and any darkness,
however fluid and however
dangerous, to take the
one hand you know
belongs in yours.*

—David Whyte
(from The Truelove in The *House of Belonging*)

Rising from the Well

(for Elisabeth)

> *Blessed are those who have not seen*
> *yet still believe.*
>
> —Gospel of John

I wrote this poem for you
Long before we met
I composed a dream of white silk
On a keyboard of ivory flesh

Only fools play hide and seek
When the secret is in open view
My heart came out of hiding
When I found the mystery in you

Take the road out of Cill Ronain
and turn right to follow the lower road,
An Bothar O Thuaidh,
turning slow like a river
into the glistening Irish Sea.
The ruins of Teampall Chiarain are on your left,
its roof ascended to heaven long ago
but the ancient walls stand in noble stillness.
The stones remember the wailing,
assailing winds full of rain, sand, and fury,

jagged waves of the copper sea torn up
from trough to crest and thrashed
against the temple walls.
But this luminous frame embodies a more fierce and
unyielding presence,
rootedness of sacred stone deep into earth.

The blessed hawthorn is in bloom,
wreathed in a mist of white flowers,
unimaginably subtle and sweet
whispers of fragrance,
colorful ribbons tied to the branches
by pilgrims who came with
prayers of love and faith,
leaving behind a most slender form of their dreams
dissolving slowly
as they are carried to God.

This is where I kneeled
at the holy well of St. Ciarán,
An Tobar Chiaráin,
entrance into the womb of the goddess Danu.
Here the prayers of the Celtic ancestors
are still heard in the bubbles that rise to the surface,
the cool living water brings new life
to all who kneel to discover in their small reflected faces,

the immensity of their souls.
It was here
at that deepening silver spring,
the Lady of the Well rose up,
ivory flesh in white lace
clinging to her elegant wetness,
revealing what God reveals;
soft shapliness of the ocean's body,
in delicate definition
smooth flow of shoreline
curvature of hidden coves…
The moon's sleek contour
of flesh,
translucent gown,
ripening fullness.
I fell to my knees imagining
the mystery of what she holds back.
In such outpouring of beauty
the moon threw down her silver light
upon the altar of Temple Ciarán.
The Lady of the Well
threw my mind down
off its throne.

In the middle of this life
my sailing ship fell deaf to the wind,
lost its heart and vision
washed upon this Irish coast
into the mystery of your harbor.

Finding you was remembering you
like a dizzying déjà vu,
when sunlight glides across water
and the dazzle sketches
a long-forgotten language
my ancestors once spoke,
and I must remember it now because
destiny is unfolding,
my life depends on deciphering
these fragile lines
painted in the archaic mind like constellations
telling a story of a time yet to come
when although I had done nothing to earn such a blessing
I would meet you one day
where water and light
share each other's body.
In breathless reverie,
my heart would break open
with the urgency of loving fiercely
the one I was born to love.
You arrived like the long-awaited
warm winds of spring,
slow work of God,
enduring faith in what is not yet seen,
your wild blond curls
blossoming like fragrances
found only in exotic night gardens.
I drifted like a boat unmoored
into the intimate blue sea of your eyes.

At the wellspring of love,
the flowers of the hawthorn
throw off their scent
like a circle of flames
around your luminous body.
The bell of Temple Ciarán is chiming
across the meadow and out to sea
like smoke rising in the wild heights of longing.
This Emerald Isle is breaking free
like our love that was meant to be,
carrying us higher into the white heat of the stars,
twin flames of belonging.

BODY PRAYER

Breath is rising…and mind is riding
on the same expanding wave that so lovingly fills
all the rooms of your precious body with the fragrance of lilacs,
stirs the fleshy green flames of the tree,
blows across the lavender sea,
and lifts the full moon gently
up over the blue mountains
and through the silver sky.
This radiance holds nothing back,
illuminates like the love of the saints
and gives its brilliance away completely,
even as it sinks and is absorbed
into the deep ocean body
that is you.

A straight line infinitely projected
Becomes a circle,
It returns to the starting point.
You must end where you begin;
As you begin in God
You must go back to God.

—Swami Vivekananda

Acknowledgements

In a letter written in 1914, Rainer Maria Rilke proposed that the poet's true motivation is not in making oneself understood to the reader but an urgent calling to inwardness in order to understand one's own depths, essence of feeling-images, and movements of spirit. For the past three years writing has been my way of laying bare the truth of all that has been hidden within myself. The old ethic of denial and repression (fracturing of self) has been replaced by a new ethic of shadow recognition, acknowledgement and integration into the totality of the self (where everything belongs).

I witnessed the emergence of repressed vulnerability, grief, anger and shame. These aspects of me were unruly like animals from unfamiliar provinces. These poems are my attempts to befriend and understand the true nature of these animals.

Through the process of constructing these poems I have often felt deconstructed as if torn apart in a purgatory state. At times the breakthrough into clear light felt like I was floating in luminosity - a radical lightness of being – a state of liberation from my own false beliefs. I have translated the despair of soul loss and the devastation of a body unbalanced by mangled energy. Deeply personal explorations of this kind might be seen as self-indulgent. Deep honesty, spiritual courage and the encounter with our most sensitive and intuitive nature are not generally regarded as worthwhile projects in our materialist culture.

Poetry is redemption. Words are like the thread of Ariadne that leads us out of soul loss into the fields of liberation. Writing has been my soul's natural inclination to tell its story of lost and found, darkness and light, the universal myth of falling into ignorance and rising into resonance with the divine. The ability to stay open to imagery and emotion could not have been endured without the genuine support and encouragement of so many people. All the love I could ever ask for has been present for me throughout this project.

I have been blessed with an opportunity to study closely with two brilliant spiritual masters, Traleg Kyabgon Rinpoche and Father Aristide Bruni. They both awakened different aspects of my soul through their various teachings on compassion, unconditioned presence, the slow and patient waiting for inborn enlightenment to blossom. I do not know how to express my gratitude for the gift of witnessing their living examples of embodiment of luminous bliss.

Brother Don Bisson is a gifted teacher of contemplative Christianity and a true healer in the tradition of Jungian Spiritual Direction. This book would not have been possible without his intuitive and compassionate skills in "holding the container" of my spiritual doubt, despair, dreams and breathtaking emergence of awareness.

I wish to thank my editor, Catharine Clarke, who taught me that poetry matters, that I matter, and the endless winding search for word, meaning and essence is the path that really matters. Her support took the form of extraordinary compassion, sensitivity to the movement of spirit, and deep respect for the raw vulnerability of unconscious material newly emerging.

I wish to thank the spiritual imprint of my ancestors, my family of belonging, my two wonderful children.

Most importantly I wish to thank my wife and muse Elisabeth for calling me back repeatedly to the radical presence of love when I have too often drifted off into self-absorption.

Craig Ciarán Lennon
January, 2017

About the Author

Craig Ciarán Lennon, Ph.D. is a clinical psychologist and spiritual director practicing in the tradition of Jungian Depth Psychology. His workshops combine poetry, myth and active imagination in the exploration of a variety of psychospiritual themes:

- Cultivating unlimited compassion for your Shadow
- Celtic Spirituality and the living flame of Nature
- Odysseus and the Soul's voyage home
- Meditation practices in the mystical traditions of Christianity and Buddhism

To order books or to contact Dr. Lennon:

- lennonpsychology.com
- lennonpsychology@gmail.com
- P.O. Box 730, Catskill, New York 12414

CPSIA information can be obtained
at www.ICGtesting.com
Printed in the USA
FSOW03n0956010217
30255FS

9 780997 896404